Denmark

Denmark

BY R. CONRAD STEIN

Enchantment of the World™
Second Series

CHILDREN'S PRESS®

An Imprint of Scholastic Inc.

Frontispiece: **Frederiksborg Castle**

Consultant: Christine Ingebritsen, PhD, Professor of Scandinavian Studies,
University of Washington, Seattle, Washington
Please note: All statistics are as up-to-date as possible at the time of publication.

Book production by The Design Lab

Library of Congress Cataloging-in-Publication Data
Names: Stein, R. Conrad, author.
Title: Denmark / by R. Conrad Stein.
Description: New York : Children's Press, [2017] | Series: Enchantment of the world |
    Includes bibliographical references and index.
Identifiers: LCCN 2016025114 | ISBN 9780531220832 (library binding)
Subjects: LCSH: Denmark—Juvenile literature.
Classification: LCC DL109 .S8 2017 | DDC 948.9—dc23
LC record available at https://lccn.loc.gov/2016025114

1 2 3 4 5 6 7 8 9 10 R 26 25 24 23 22 21 20 19 18 17

Building in Aarhus

Contents

Left to right: **Aalborg, red deer, ancient bronze helmets, Frederick's Church, Easter eggs**

CHAPTER 1

A Happy Kingdom

IN 2016, THE UNITED NATIONS (UN), AN INTERNATIONAL organization devoted to promoting peace and cooperation between countries, conducted a study on happiness worldwide. The study concluded that Danes, the people from the northern European nation of Denmark, are the happiest people on earth. The United States ranked thirteenth on the happiness scale. Earlier studies, completed by the UN and other organizations, reached the same conclusion: Denmark is a happy country.

Many factors influence the Danish spirit of well-being. One factor that most certainly does not help, however, is the weather. Danish winters are cloudy and gloomy. They last from a chilly November through a drizzly April.

Opposite: **Brightly colored houses line the canal in the Nyhavn neighborhood of Copenhagen. Many of the houses date to the seventeenth century.**

People's financial situation plays a role in their sense of well-being. Denmark is prosperous, but not everyone feels rich. The day-to-day cost of living is high, yet Danes enjoy one of the highest standards of living in the world. This economic well-being comes despite the fact that the nation's sandy soil is not very fertile and the land has few resources. Denmark's prosperity comes from its skilled workers, who turn out world-famous furniture, silverware, foods, toys, and porcelain products.

Many people believe that the Danish people's good feelings stem from a sense of economic security. Danes pay high taxes and in return they receive extensive benefits throughout their lives. The Danish system of government provides an umbrella that covers all. In Denmark, no one goes hungry or suffers the extremes of poverty. Poor people are given work or assistance. There is no tuition for most college students, and most health care costs are paid by the government or employers. Although some criticize this welfare state, few Danes express any desire to change what they say is an ideal system of government.

Elderly Danes relax in a park in Copenhagen. On average, Danish people can expect to live eighty-one years.

CHAPTER 2

Land and Sea

TAKE A QUICK GLANCE AT A MAP OF NORTHERN EUROPE, and Denmark appears to be a peninsula, a finger of land, jutting into the North Sea. Give the map a closer look and it becomes apparent that Denmark also includes two large islands and dozens of smaller ones hugging the peninsula. Denmark's only land neighbor is Germany to the south. Including all its islands, Denmark spreads over 16,570 square miles (42,916 square kilometers). This makes the nation only slightly bigger than the U.S. state of Maryland. If Denmark were part of the United States, it would rank forty-first in size among the fifty states.

Denmark is the smallest nation in the northern European mainland and one of the smallest in the world. Danes are proud of the fact that their country is small. The Danish poet Piet Hein once wrote:

Opposite: **Bornholm, a Danish island in the Baltic Sea, features a jagged, rocky coast.**

A lighthouse stands guard at one of Denmark's many peaceful beaches.

Denmark seen from foreign land
Looks but like a grain of sand.
Denmark as we Danes conceive it
Is so big you won't believe it

Why not let us compromise
About Denmark's proper size?
Which will truly please us all
Since it's greater than it's small.

Denmark's Geographic Features

Area: 16,570 square miles (42,916 sq km)

Greatest Distance North to South: 225 miles (362 km)

Greatest Distance East to West: 250 miles (402 km)

Highest Elevation: Yding Skovhoj, 568 feet (173 m) above sea level

Lowest Elevation: 23 feet (7 m) below sea level

Longest River: Gudena, about 100 miles (160 km)

Largest Lake: Arreso, about 16 square miles (41 sq km)

Length of Coastline: Including islands, some 4,500 miles (7,200 km)

Average High Temperature: In Copenhagen, 36°F (2°C) in January, 72°F (22°C) in July

Average Low Temperature: In Copenhagen, 28°F (-2°C) in January, 57°F (14°C) in July

Average Annual Precipitation: 24 inches (61 cm)

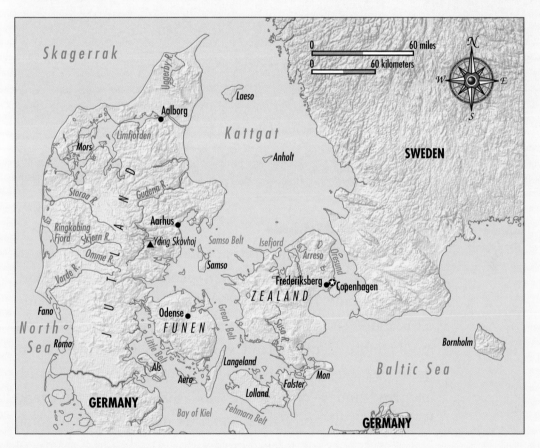

Mainland and Islands

Denmark is part of the northern European region known as Scandinavia. The nation's main peninsula, called Jutland, comprises some 70 percent of the total land area. The largest island is Zealand, home to about two million people. The most remote Danish island is Bornholm, which lies in the Baltic Sea some 80 miles (130 kilometers) east of the Danish mainland and is closer to Poland than it is to Denmark. Funen, Lolland, and Falster are other major islands. In total, Danish territory includes about four hundred islands. Many of the islands are uninhabited, and some are mere rocks poking above the waters.

As a country made up of a peninsula and islands, Denmark features a lengthy coastline. Visitors can find gentle beaches and stark, rocky cliffs along the seacoast. Many small inlets, called fjords, cut into the coastline. The fjords often have peaceful sandy beaches that draw swimmers and picnickers. Including the many islands, the country's coastline extends some 4,500 miles (7,200 km). This means the seacoast of tiny Denmark is roughly the same distance as from San Francisco, California, to New York City and halfway back again.

Most Danes live an easy walk from the sea, and almost every town of importance serves as a port. No place in Denmark is more than 35 miles (56 km) from the coast. The sea does not just surround Denmark, it is part of the nation's blood. Throughout Denmark's history, seafaring has been central to the people.

Shape of the Land

No one visits Denmark to see majestic mountains. There simply are no mountains there. The highest point in Denmark is Yding Skovhoj, which rises only 568 feet (173 meters) above sea level, and it can hardly be called a hill. Thousands of years ago, an ice age gripped the earth, and what is now Denmark was buried under enormous glaciers. The mountains of ice moved slowly over the surface and ground Denmark into what it is today: a country almost as flat as a tabletop.

Denmark has few large rivers or lakes. The longest river is the Gudena, which runs about 100 miles (160 km), and the largest lake is the Arreso. Many fjords play the role that lakes play in other countries, giving people the opportunity to fish or go swimming.

Kayakers float down the Gudena, which flows from central Jutland toward the northeast.

Denmark's largest inland body of water is Limfjorden, which is located near the northern tip of Jutland. From the land, Limfjorden looks like a lake, but it is actually a fjord since it is open to the sea on two sides. A thousand years ago, seafaring traders and raiders known as the Vikings docked ships there. Today, Limfjorden is a peaceful vacation spot in the summer.

The Other Denmark

Greenland and the Faroe Islands are in the north Atlantic Ocean, and both are possessions of the Kingdom of Denmark. Long ago, both places were visited by brave Scandinavian sailors. Eventually, possession of the islands fell to the Danish government. Today, Greenland and the Faroes are independent states with close ties to Denmark. Technically they are listed as provinces, not colonies. Both island nations have home rule, and residents elect their own officials. The Kingdom of Denmark conducts foreign affairs for Greenland and the Faroes, and the two countries are protected by the Danish military.

Greenland is the largest island in the world. (Australia is bigger, but it is considered a continent, not an island.) Viking explorer Leif Erikson established a colony on Greenland in 985 CE. Most of the colonists came from Iceland and lived as near neighbors with the Inuit people who were native to the island. Erikson and other leaders hoped to attract more settlers, so they told a little lie. They named the island Greenland to lure farmers to the land. In fact, Greenland was

Many buildings on the Faroe Islands have sod roofs—a layer of earth covered with grass. These roofs provide excellent insulation, protecting the buildings from the heat and the cold.

covered by ice and it was all but impossible to grow anything there. Settlers soon discovered this hoax, and Greenland never had a large European population. Today, Greenland is home to only about fifty-seven thousand people, making it the least densely populated country on earth.

The Faroes are a group of eighteen small islands that lie in the North Atlantic about midway between Norway and Iceland. Rugged Scandinavian settlers began living on the islands as early as 800 CE. It is believed the early settlers probably raised sheep, because the word *Faroes* is closely related to a Danish term meaning "islands of sheep." In 2015, the Faroes had a population of 48,700, most of whom are ethnic Scandinavians. To this day, the islanders raise sheep.

Looking at Denmark's Cities

Copenhagen, founded in 1167, is Denmark's capital and biggest city, with a population of nearly 600,000 in 2016. Aarhus (below), on the east coast of Jutland, is the nation's second-largest city, home to about 265,000 people. Aarhus is one of the busiest port cities in northern Europe, regularly receiving huge cargo ships and cruise ships. Every year, the city hosts major music festivals, including the eight-day Aarhus International Jazz Festival.

Odense, Denmark's third-largest city, with a population of more than 175,000, rests on the island of Funen. Its most famous citizen was the beloved storyteller Hans Christian Andersen. Statues in Odense parks celebrate the many wonderful characters Andersen created, such as the Little Mermaid. Odense is home to many magnificent old churches. St. Canute's is a soaring Gothic cathedral.

Aalborg (above), which has a population of more than 110,000, is an industrial and cultural center in northern Jutland. It is home to Aalborg University, which serves some seventeen thousand students. The city's largest company is Telenor, a mobile phone maker. Aalborg's Old City Hall dates to 1762.

Frederiksberg, home to more than 100,000 people, was founded just west of Copenhagen in 1651 by King Frederick III. Over the years, Copenhagen expanded and swallowed up Frederiksberg, making it seem like a neighborhood of the Danish capital. Still, residents of Frederiksberg cling to their separate identity. The city has many parks and gardens, and is the site of the Copenhagen Zoo.

CHAPTER 3

A Lovely Land

THERE IS A LOVELY LAND
With spreading, shady beeches
Near Baltic's salty strand.
Its hills and valleys gently fall,
Its ancient name is Denmark
    From "There Is a Lovely Land,"
    one of Denmark's two national anthems

Green Denmark

Don't expect to see thick forests in Denmark. People have been living on the land for thousands of years, and the land has been farmed for many hundreds of years. Little land remains where nature has not been disturbed. Still, patches of wilderness survive, and they are protected by the Danish government. Cutting down large trees is forbidden. Hunting is carefully controlled. Because it is protected, wildlife flourishes in Denmark.

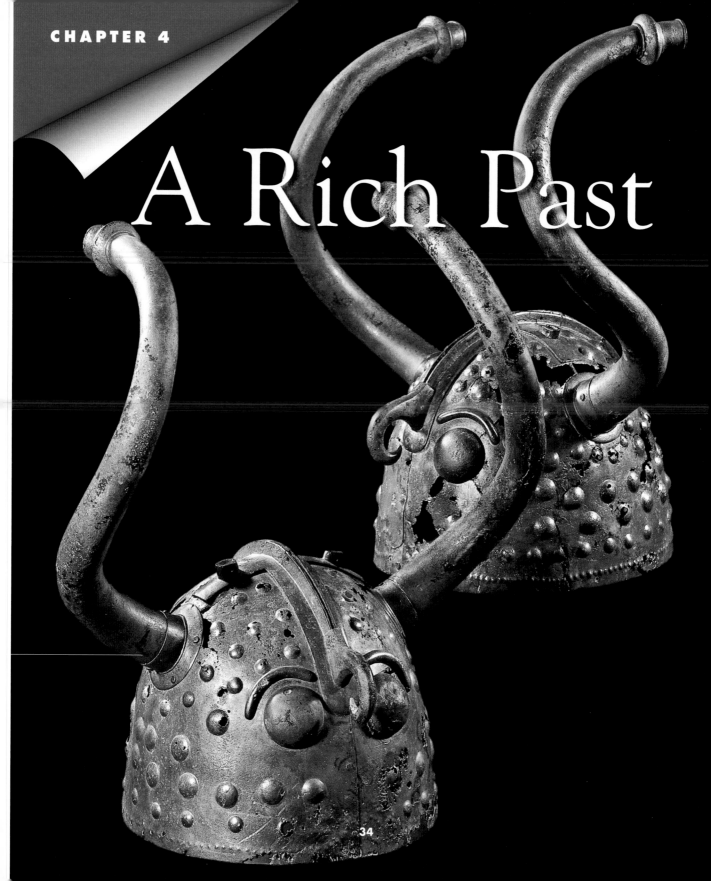

CHAPTER 4

A Rich Past

34

MANY THOUSANDS OF YEARS AGO, WHEN ALL OF northern Europe was experiencing an ice age, great glaciers covered Denmark and most of the Scandinavian countries. Because so much of the ocean waters were turned into ice, sea level was about 300 feet (90 m) lower than it is today. If you had lived in ice-covered Denmark during the Ice Age, you could have walked to what is now Sweden or Norway. In fact, you could have taken a long and chilly walk to Great Britain over fields of ice. Despite these harsh conditions, men and women lived or at least passed through the land that would later become Denmark. Evidence suggests that some hardy souls inhabited Denmark one hundred thousand years ago. Those first people built no permanent structures, and they soon retreated to the south. Perhaps the climate was too harsh.

Opposite: **These bronze helmets were found on the island of Zealand. They are more than two thousand years old.**

Early people in what is now Denmark survived by hunting and fishing.

Then, around fourteen thousand years ago, the Ice Age moderated, and bands of people moved from the south into northern Europe. These men and women stayed, beginning a long history of continuous settlement. The ancient people survived by hunting and fishing. People began farming in the region as early as 3000 BCE. About 500 CE, a group called the Danes migrated from Sweden to Denmark and gave the people of Denmark a name.

Monk with a Mission

According to legend, an Irish monk named Saint Brendan of Clonfert was the first European to live on the Faroe Islands. Perhaps he arrived as early as the 400s CE. Saint Brendan was looking for an isolated place to meditate and worship God. No one knows if the story of Brendan's travels to the Faroes is true or a mythical tale. If true, the saint found total privacy in the isolated islands.

The Vikings

The sea was vital to the Danes. Beginning in the 700s, sailors from Denmark united with others from Sweden and Norway to form loose-knit societies that became known as Vikings. The word *Vikings* might have derived from a northern European word, *vic*, meaning "inlet" or "bay." In England, the Viking seamen were called the Northmen, or Norsemen, or simply the Danes. English historians did not distinguish the country of origin of the people from the north, but it is assumed many hailed from present-day Denmark. Whatever their name, they were feared. The Vikings were warriors as well as sailors. They conquered, they plundered, and they enslaved some victims. Churches in England regularly offered up a special prayer, "God, deliver us from the fury of the Northmen."

England was the Vikings' frequent target. Attacks on English coastal villages began in the 700s and lasted for three hundred years. The English thought the invaders from the north were madmen. In battle, Viking swordsmen sometimes laughed wildly. They fought recklessly as if they had no fear of death. A common belief among the Vikings held that a man who was killed in battle would immediately be carried by beautiful maidens, called Valkyries, up to Valhalla, a heavenly realm. The Vikings worshipped many gods, but the highest of their deities was Odin, lord of war.

In the early 1000s, the Vikings stormed London and pulled down the London Bridge, an action that gave rise to the children's song "London Bridge Is Falling Down." For decades, the Vikings controlled a large section of England,

Many Viking ships were powered by both oars and sails.

which they called Danelaw. In 1013, the Danish prince Sweyn Forkbeard seized control and named himself king of England and Denmark.

The Vikings were also active in France. In 845, a Danish leader named Ragnar took 120 ships up the Seine River and occupied half of Paris. A tense stalemate followed. French armies camped on one side of the Seine River while the Danes formed ranks on the other. Then, in full view of the French soldiers, Ragnar's men hanged all the prisoners on their side

The World's Finest Ships

Key to the Vikings' success were their swift and powerful ships. The Vikings were by far the best shipbuilders in Europe. Their ships held about forty people and were propelled by oars as well as sails. When building these vessels, master Viking carpenters fitted planks tightly together to form sturdy hulls. The hulls enabled the ships to plow through the treacherous waves of the North Atlantic. Today, near the town of Roskilde on Zealand, stands the Viking Ship Museum. The museum houses five ships discovered on the seafloor in 1962. The ships date back to the years 1030 and 1042. It is believed they were sunk deliberately by their crews to prevent them from falling into the hands of an enemy.

of the Seine. The French king paid Ragnar a fortune in silver to withdraw from his capital city. Ragnar accepted the sum and left. The ransom was called Danegelds, or Danish money.

Yet it is incorrect to think of the Vikings strictly as pirates and warriors. The Vikings were also bold seamen and the greatest explorers in Europe at the time. During the Viking era, Danish ships ventured into the Atlantic and discovered Iceland, Greenland, and the Faroe Islands. Some ships even reached North America and established settlements in Newfoundland, in what is now Canada. The Vikings, not Christopher Columbus and his crew, were the first Europeans to reach the Americas. Viking ships also sailed into the Mediterranean Sea and Viking parties trekked eastward into Russia. The travelers brought goods that they traded in far-flung parts of the world.

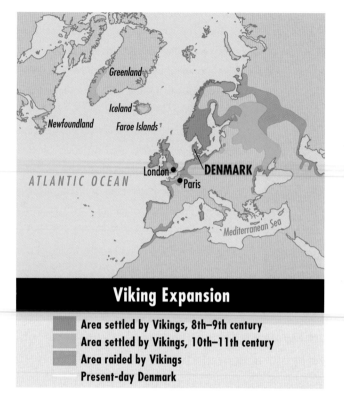

Viking Expansion

Area settled by Vikings, 8th–9th century
Area settled by Vikings, 10th–11th century
Area raided by Vikings
Present-day Denmark

The Vikings were also great poets and storytellers. Many of their stories told of heroic adventures at sea. Today these stories are preserved in Norse sagas. Some Viking stories are recorded on rune stones, standing stones that were often used to mark the graves of important leaders. The rune stones are carved with pictures as well as words. These stones are found in every Scandinavian country.

The Viking age lasted from roughly 750 to 1050. At the time, Denmark was made up of many small provinces ruled by chieftains or princes. In 950, a king named Harald Bluetooth rose to power over all of Denmark and united the many provinces. Bluetooth also brought Christianity to the land. Gone were the Viking warrior gods such as Odin and Thor. The new religion was gentler than the old. Christianity helped tame the Vikings, much to the relief of the English and other neighbors.

The Danish Empire

Valdemar I, also known as Valdemar the Great, became king of Denmark in 1146. He fought his rivals and completed the

King Harald Bluetooth erected this large stone honoring his conquest of Denmark and the conversion of Danes to Christianity. The stone includes a depiction of Jesus Christ.

process of uniting the provinces and forming a powerful kingdom. King Valdemar was aided by a priest known as Absalon. Unlike Danish leaders in the past, Absalon was both a scholar and a warrior. He urged Valdemar to forgive rather than punish those who fought against him in the war. With peace prevailing in the land, Absalon became an archbishop, a powerful figure in the church. Under his guidance, many churches and monasteries were built and schools were founded to promote Danish civilization.

Christian IV, the king of Denmark, fought in the Thirty Years' War. He and his troops were defeated at the Battle of Lutter in what is now northern Germany.

Union, the North Atlantic colonies of Iceland, Greenland, and the Faroe Islands fell under the rule of Denmark.

Religion and War

For more than a thousand years, Roman Catholicism was the only Christian religion practiced in Europe. The Catholic Church held great power over Europeans. Church leaders amassed fortunes through the practice of selling indulgences (the forgiveness of sin) to parishioners. The indulgences were paid in the form of gold or in funds used to build mighty church buildings. The church was like a second government, often overshadowing the power of kings. Then, on October 31, 1517, a German priest named Martin Luther nailed a letter on the

King Christian IV succeeded his father in 1588, but since he was a child he didn't take the throne until 1596 at the age of nineteen. His reign lasted the longest of any Danish monarch. He was popular with the people, and his administration contributed to the nation's prosperity.

Christian IV built up the Danish naval fleet, often personally designing the ships. He was also a musician and a poet. But the king had a fault: He believed in witchcraft and he ordered many suspected witches to be burned at the stake.

door of his church in Wittenberg, Germany. The letter listed a set of demands to change, or reform, the practices of the Roman Catholic Church.

Luther's action launched a revolution called the Protestant Reformation. In the next forty years, some northern Europeans turned away from the Catholic Church and embraced Protestant (non-Catholic) religions. In Denmark, King Christian III established Lutheranism, which followed the teachings of Martin Luther, as the country's official religion in 1536.

The Reformation triggered wars in Denmark and most of Europe. A conflict called the Thirty Years' War rocked Europe from 1618 to 1648. Warfare reached Denmark, but the most bitter religious fighting took place in Germany. There, many thousands of men and women were killed.

Warfare associated with the Reformation drained Denmark's treasury. The country taxed the upper classes to pay for its army. Many nobles refused to pay. To punish them, King Frederick III (who ruled from 1648 to 1670) instituted King's Law of 1665, giving the monarch virtually all the nation's political power. Five years later, Christian V became king, and he continued the policy of absolute monarchy.

Colonies Overseas

In the seventeenth century, many European nations established overseas colonies in Asia, Africa, and the Americas. Beginning in 1660, the Danish East India Company founded a handful of outposts on the coast of India. Denmark also took control of the Caribbean islands of St. Thomas, St. John, and St. Croix, which comprise the Virgin Islands. With the labor of thousands of enslaved men and women from Africa, the Danes in the Caribbean ran profitable sugar and tobacco plantations.

In 1869, the British drove Denmark out of India. Denmark held the Virgin Islands until 1917, when it sold them to the United States for $25 million. The capital city of Charlotte Amalie on St. Thomas still bears the name of a long-ago Danish queen.

Danish commoners reluctantly welcomed the policy because an all-powerful king brought a measure of peace to the land. Kings continued to rule as absolute monarchs until 1848.

Progress and Change

During the period of absolute monarchy, kings kept the power of the nobles in check, and commoners made genuine progress. From the time of the Vikings, farmworkers, called serfs, lived almost like slaves under their masters, who were wealthy land-owners. Farmworkers were housed in dismal central buildings, always under the watchful eye of the nobles. Gradually the serfdom laws ended. The serfs were allowed to build their own cottages and buy small patches of land. Rural Denmark began to work as it does today, as a series of small, family-owned farms.

Cities were also developing. Copenhagen had begun as

a tiny fishing village, but boasting a fine natural harbor, it emerged as a trading center. The name Copenhagen comes from an ancient word meaning "merchants' haven."

War swept through Europe in the early 1800s. Denmark sided with France in its war against the United Kingdom, and the people paid a heavy price for this choice. In 1807, the British fleet sailed into Copenhagen's harbor, and their cannons bombarded the defenseless city for four days. Copenhagen was set ablaze, many buildings were reduced to rubble, and at least two thousand civilians were killed. After the bombardment, thirty thousand British landed and occupied the capital.

Crowds gather to hear a speech by Frederick III in Copenhagen in 1660.

The British bombardment of Copenhagen set the city ablaze. More than a thousand buildings were burned.

When the British finally withdrew from Danish waters, they took with them 170 ships that had once belonged to the Danish navy.

The war weakened the power of the king. In 1848, the public demanded change, and King Frederick VII was forced to accept a new constitution. Government power now rested in a two-house parliament. The era of the absolute monarchy was over. Also, Denmark lost territory to its south as the region of Schleswig was taken over by Germany.

Ultimately, Denmark benefited from this loss. With the borders established more or less as they are now, the government concentrated on developing Jutland into a strong agricultural region. Industrialization also bloomed in the early

1800s as Denmark built railroads connecting every corner of its land. Aided by the railroads, people moved from rural areas to the cities.

Life for the commoners steadily improved. Early in the 1800s, measures were passed requiring all children to attend primary school. Denmark was the first country in Europe to educate everyone, even its poorest citizens.

Danish children practice lessons at a village school in 1881.

Twentieth-Century Denmark

The first half of the twentieth century was a brutal period of war for Europe and much of the world. World War I began in 1914 and lasted four bloody years. The war was characterized by trenches stretching across Europe. Under a rain of machine gun and artillery fire, some nine million soldiers and seven million civilians died. Denmark declared itself neutral at the start of the conflict and managed to maintain its neutrality even though it was often threatened by its southern neighbor, Germany.

Unemployment blighted life in Denmark during the world-wide Great Depression of the 1930s. Germany suffered even harsher times in the depression years. Looking for a savior, the Germans turned to a fiery speaker, Adolf Hitler, who headed the Nazi Party. Hitler became leader of Germany in 1933, and immediately built up the nation's military. In 1939, Germany attacked Poland, marking the beginning of World War II.

"All of Denmark"

When Germany occupied Denmark during World War II, King Christian X took daily rides on his horse, Jubilee, through the streets of Copenhagen. He rode by himself, without a bodyguard or a groom to take care of the horse. According to an often-told story, a German soldier once asked a Danish boy, "Why doesn't the king at least have a bodyguard with him?" The boy answered, "All of Denmark is his bodyguard."

Once more Denmark declared neutrality. But Hitler refused to recognize Germany's northern neighbor as a neutral nation. On April 9, 1940, German forces marched into Denmark. After just two hours of combat, the Danish government surrendered. The German army at the time was the strongest in the world, and Danish leaders knew resistance would be futile.

During the war, Denmark was an occupied country. At first an uneasy peace prevailed between the Danish people and the German forces. King Christian X was allowed to keep his

German forces march through Copenhagen in 1940, just days after the German army gained control of Denmark.

Controversial Cartoons

Kurt Westergaard is a Danish school teacher and a cartoonist. In 2005, Westergaard drew a cartoon depicting Muhammad, the prophet of the religion Islam, wearing a bomb in his turban. Muslims throughout the world denounced Westergaard for insulting Muhammad. Westergaard claimed he was acting on his right of free speech under Danish law. This clash between free speech and Muslim sensitivities rocked Denmark. There were protests around the world, and Danish embassies were attacked in several Muslim countries. Danish exports to Muslim countries also dropped.

Danes, the services they received in exchange for the taxes made the expense well worth it.

Denmark has a close relationship with other countries in Europe, but Danes remain committed to maintaining their sovereignty. Many European countries use the same currency, called the euro, but in 2000, Danish voters rejected the euro, so the country continues to use its traditional currency, the Danish krone.

In recent decades, immigration has become a major issue for the Danish people. In the 1960s, the nation faced a labor shortage and leaders encouraged immigration. The people who came, called guest workers, at first were mainly from Turkey and Pakistan. In the early 2000s, immigrants arrived from Iraq and Somalia. Many of these immigrants are Muslims. Integrating these newcomers into Danish society has sometimes posed problems. Immigrants have complained they are being discriminated against, and some Danes feel like there are too many newcomers. Some Danes have taken their grievances to the election booths. In 2015, the Danish Peoples' Party, which opposes further immigration, received the second-highest number of votes in a general election. The issue of how to handle immigration remains unsettled in Denmark.

Tens of thousands of refugees have arrived in Denmark from Syria and other war-torn countries in recent years.

CHAPTER 5

For the People

DENMARK IS A CONSTITUTIONAL MONARCHY. THIS means that the nation has a king or a queen and also a constitution. The constitution contains written laws that hold greater power than the monarch. Queen Margrethe is respected and loved. In Denmark it can be said that the queen reigns, but she does not rule. The constitution is the highest authority, providing rules under which the government operates. Under Denmark's constitution, the power to run the country falls to the parliament.

Opposite: **In 2015, Danes gathered in front of Christiansborg Palace to celebrate the one hundredth anniversary of Danish women gaining the right to vote.**

Running the Government

The nation's parliament is called the Folketing. It is a one-house legislature whose job is to make laws. The parliament is made up of 179 members, four of whom represent Greenland and the Faroe Islands. Each member is elected to a four-year term.

The art of compromise is essential in the Folketing, because as many as ten political parties are active in the country. Since the beginning of the twentieth century, no single party has held a majority in parliament. Legislation is passed when several parties get together and form a coalition govern-

The Danish parliament, supreme court, and prime minister's office are all located in Christiansborg Palace.

to the prime minister. The cabinet ministers are often members of the same party as the prime minister.

The highest court in the land is the Supreme Court. It reviews cases handled by lower courts. Many cases begin in district courts. More serious cases are tried in high courts.

Caring for the People

Denmark is one of the most prosperous countries on earth. People eat well, live in adequate housing, and enjoy excellent health care. Yet Danes also pay high taxes. Some people pay more than half of their earnings. This can make it difficult to accumulate a lot of wealth, but since the government provides high quality and abundant services, it is less necessary than

The Danish National Anthem

Denmark has two official national anthems. The anthem most often heard is "There Is a Lovely Land." The second anthem, "King Christian Stood by the Lofty Mast," is associated with the monarch and is played when the queen visits a school or government office. "There Is a Lovely Land," with words by Adam Gottlob Oehlenschlager and music by Hans Ernst Kroyer, has been recognized as a national anthem since 1844.

Danish lyrics

Der er et yndigt land,
det star med brede boge
naer salten osterstrand;
det bugter sig i bakke, dal,
det hedder gamle Danmark,
og det er Frejas Sal.

Der sad i fordums tid
de harniskklaedte kaemper,
udhvilede fra strid;
sa drog de frem til fjenders men
nu hvile deres bene
bag hojens bautasten.

Det land endnu er skont,
thi bla sig soen baelter,
og lovet star sa gront;
og aedle kvinder, skonne mo'r
og maend og raske svende
bebo de danskes oer.

Hil drot og faedreland!
Hil hver en danneborger,
som virker, hvad han kan!
Vort gamle Danmark skal besta,
sa laenge bogen spejler
sin top i bolgen bla.

English translation

There is a lovely land
With spreading, shady beeches
Near Baltic's salty strand.
Its hills and valleys gently fall,
Its ancient name is Denmark
And it is Freya's hall.

There in ancient days
The armored Vikings rested
Between their bloody frays.
Then they went forth the foe to face,
Now found in stone-set barrows,
Their final resting place.

The land is still as fair
The sea as blue around it,
And peace is cherished there.
Strong men and noble women still
uphold their country's honor
With faithfulness and skill.

Praise the king and country with might
Bless every Dane at heart
For serving with no fright.
The Viking kingdom for Danes is true
With fields and waving beeches
By a sea so blue.

in other parts of the world. In Denmark, the government has made a bottom step below which no one is allowed to fall. The pain of poverty and the excesses of wealth are trimmed, so everyone lives a more or less middle-class life.

The Danish system protects a person from infancy to old age, but does this system stifle a person's individuality? How could a worker who pays half his wages in taxes ever save enough money to start his or her own business? Danes continue to discuss these questions.

Daycare workers take children for a walk in Copenhagen. In Denmark, the government pays for most daycare costs.

Governing the Other Denmark

Greenland and the Faroe Islands enjoy a special status. They are states under the Danish Crown, but they are not colonies of Denmark. Greenland has two ministers in the Danish parliament, and the Faroes have two ministers. Both states have independent local governments that run their school systems and local police forces. Unlike colonies, both states are free to leave the Danish kingdom anytime they wish. The question of independence is frequently posed on ballots, but there has been no strong independence movement.

Nuuk is the capital of Greenland and its largest city, with a population of about seventeen thousand.

Copenhagen is the nation's largest city, home to 591,481 people in 2016. It is the center of finance, culture, and trade. A visit to Copenhagen makes clear Denmark's connection to the sea. The Danish capital is a collection of harbors, piers, and islands. The sea is all around.

The city center and its historic heart is found at the City Hall Square. The City Hall itself features statues of polar bears that appear to be climbing the walls to reach the roof. The great white bears signify Denmark's attachment to Greenland. Near City Hall Square is the main train station and an amusement park called Tivoli Gardens (right). A pedestrian walkway called Stroget Street leads away from the square. It is lined with restaurants and stores. Stroget Street is a favorite gathering place for street musicians and clowns.

Amalienborg Palace is the official home of the royal family. Several wings of the palace are open to the public. Crowds inside admire the paintings and sculptures. A tradition holds at the palace: If the flag is flying it means the queen is home. Look up at the balcony, and perhaps you will see her waving to the crowds. Every day at noon a marching band appears, and a colorful changing of the guard ceremony is held outside the palace main doors.

Parliament, the seat of government, meets at Christiansborg Palace. The current building opened in 1928, but a castle has stood on this spot since 1167. In addition to the parliament, the palace houses the office of the prime minister and the Danish Supreme Court. Visitors to Christiansborg must take off their shoes at the door and put on special slippers, as the floor is delicate and scratches easily.

In a square next to Christiansborg Palace is a statue of Absalon on horseback (opposite). Absalon, an archbishop and a warrior, is credited with founding Copenhagen.

Nearby stands the Round Tower. Built in 1637, it rises as high as an eight-story building. Inside the tower is a spiral walkway that guests can climb to enjoy a commanding view of the city.

Home to the nation's finest schools and museums, Copenhagen is the cultural center of Denmark. The University of Copenhagen, founded in 1479, is the oldest university in the nation. Copenhagen's National Museum of Denmark traces Danish history from Ice Age hunting groups who roamed the land fourteen thousand years ago to contemporary times. The National Gallery of Denmark, in the capital's center, displays thousands of paintings and sculptures.

No visit to Copenhagen is complete without a stop to see the Little Mermaid statue that sits at the harbor. It is Copenhagen's most famous landmark. Some say it is the most photographed statue of Denmark.

Copenhagen

CHAPTER 6

On the Job

DENMARK HAS FEW NATURAL RESOURCES. ITS farmland requires the heavy use of fertilizer to yield crops. Despite these shortcomings, the nation has a strong economy. The Danish economy benefits from lively trade, and Danish factories and farms buzz with activity.

Denmark's economic success stems in part from the Danish imagination. One success story began during the Great Depression of the 1930s, when a carpenter named Ole Kirk Christiansen lost his job. Wanting to support his family, the carpenter devised a puzzle game composed of interlocking wooden bricks. Traveling on his bicycle, he sold the game from house to house. Christiansen called the game Lego, based on the Danish words *leg godt*, mean-

Opposite: **A worker walks through a miniature Copenhagen at Legoland in Billund, Denmark, the world headquarters of the Lego company. Lego is the largest toy company in the world.**

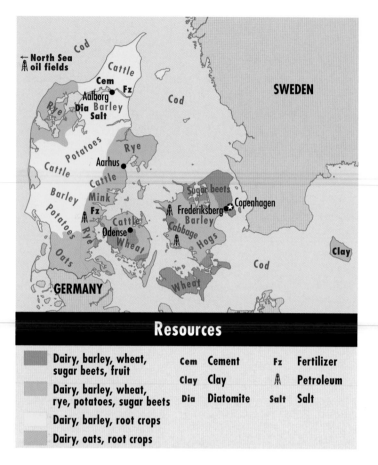

Resources

■ Dairy, barley, wheat, sugar beets, fruit	Cem	Cement	Fz	Fertilizer	
■ Dairy, barley, wheat, rye, potatoes, sugar beets	Clay	Clay	⚒	Petroleum	
	Dia	Diatomite	Salt	Salt	
■ Dairy, barley, root crops					
■ Dairy, oats, root crops					

ing "play well." In 1949, he began making his blocks out of plastics, and the internationally famous Legos were born. In 2015, the Lego company enjoyed sales of more than $5 billion. The company is still controlled by the Christiansens.

Farm Products

Farms cover about 61 percent of Denmark's total land area. Most farms are small, averaging about 100 acres (40 hectares) and they tend to be run by families. The farms require the use of fertilizer, and they are operated using tractors and planting and harvesting machines. Many of these devices are high tech, which means a farmer has to be part machinist and part engineer. The machines also automate farmwork, reducing the need for labor. In 2016, less than 3 percent of the nation's workforce was employed in agriculture. Major crops grown on Danish farms include wheat, barley, hay, sugar beets, cabbage, and potatoes.

For a tiny nation, Denmark is a livestock giant. Hogs are the leading farm animal, and Danish farms raise some thirty million pigs. Danish ham, bacon, and sausages are thought of as some of the tastiest in the world and are eagerly bought up on the international market. Beef cattle are also important. About 550,000 beef cattle are raised on Danish farms. More than a half million dairy cows graze fields in Denmark. Milk products, particularly Danish-made cheese, are valued abroad.

Danish farms produce enough food to feed 15 million people, or three times the country's population. Because of this, Denmark sells much of its agricultural output to other nations. Today, goods from the farms make up 20 percent of all Danish exports. Danish farm products are shipped to more than a hundred nations around the world.

What Denmark Grows, Makes, and Mines

AGRICULTURE (2013)

Minks	17,200,000 animals
Pigs	12,075,750 animals
Wheat	4,139,000 metric tons

MANUFACTURING (VALUE ADDED, 2010)

Machinery	$9,825,000,000
Chemical products	$6,637,000,000
Food products	$5,747,000,000

MINING

Oil (2014)	171,000 barrels per day
Natural gas (2014)	2,549,000,000 cubic meters
Sand and gravel (2012)	50,000,000 metric tons

Men unload a fishing boat in the Faroe Islands.

Fishing

Surrounded by the sea, Danes have always turned to fish for food and for export goods. About twenty thousand Danes work in the fishing industry. Esbjerg, Thyboron, and Hanstholm are leading ports for fishing vessels. More fishing ports operate on

Fish for Furs

Industries feed other industries in Denmark. Scrap fish, those that are not fit for human consumption, are sold to mink farms. There are no wild mink scurrying around forests, but Denmark produces about one-third of the world's mink pelts. The pelts come from some 1,500 fur farms scattered about the country. The farms also raise foxes. The animals are raised so their furs can be used to make warm and fashionable winter coats. Warm coats can also be made without killing animals, however. Many Danes are animal lovers, and they argue that raising mink simply to slaughter them for their furs is cruel.

Greenland and the Faroe Islands. The North Sea accounts for most of the catch. Primary fish caught include cod, herring, turbot, and dover sole. Danish herring salted, preserved in oil, and sold in bottles is a favorite snack everywhere.

The fishing industry prides itself on its fair practices. Every member of a fishing crew receives a share from the overall catch.

Factory Products

Danish factories produce electronic devices, high-quality furniture, machinery, paper products, and medicines. About half of the nation's factories are located in the Copenhagen

Denmark is renowned for its design and manufacture of modern furniture.

area. Leading manufactured goods include processed foods (primarily meat and dairy goods), transportation equipment, medical devices, textiles, and clothing. Food processing has long been a thriving industry, as Danish plants produce canned ham and canned fish. Carlsberg beer, which has been made in Copenhagen for more than 150 years, is sold around the world. Denmark is also home to Novo Nordisk, the world's largest manufacturer of insulin, which many people who have the dangerous disease diabetes need to take.

The United States is Denmark's largest non-European trading partner. About 6 percent of Danish industrial goods are sold to the United States. Danish-made windmills are among the most advanced in the world and are coveted by American buyers. Danish design furniture (also called Scandinavian design) is sold in stores throughout the United States and Canada. Danish furniture often features sturdy teak wood and is ideal for desks and office fixtures.

Workforce

Denmark has a workforce of about three million people. All workers enjoy generous benefits. Workers are granted as much as five weeks of vacation a year. Job security is a right. If a person loses a job, he or she is entitled to as much as two years in unemployment compensation.

The Danish workforce benefits from the country's excellent school system. Factory workers quickly learn high-tech methods to produce electronic devices and other machinery. The skills learned in school translate to the workplace. Foreign languages

Employees monitor the production of insulin at a Novo Nordisk factory in Denmark.

are taught in all schools. Danish workers are well-prepared in their ability to speak foreign languages: 80 percent of the workforce speaks English, 53 percent German, 11 percent French, and 10 percent Swedish. An ability to speak different languages helps Danish businesses work with companies and clients abroad.

Danish workers tend to be well paid. Low-skilled workers might earn $20 an hour. Yet even with a high-wage scale, foreign companies continue to build plants in Denmark. For example, Sony from Japan and Volkswagen from Germany run thriving plants in Denmark. Danish businesses can be competitive while paying good wages because the employer does not pay for extra

Money Facts

Denmark's currency is called the Danish krone. Coins come in values of a half krone and 1, 2, 5, 10, and 20 kroner. Bills come in values of 50, 100, 200, 500, and 1,000 Danish kroner. The bills are easy to tell apart. The higher the value of the bill, the larger the bill is. In addition, each denomination has a different dominant color. For example, the 100-krone bill is orange, and the 200-krone bill is green. Each bill shows a picture of a bridge on the front, while the back of the bill depicts a historical object found near the bridge. The 50-krone note shows the Sallingsund Bridge on the front, and the Skarpsalling Pot, a clay vessel dating from 3200 BCE, on the back. In 2016, 1 Danish krone equaled US$0.15, and US$1.00 equaled 6.63 kroner.

costs above basic wages. In the United States, some workers receive health insurance provided by the employer. In Denmark, health insurance is provided by the government. This helps high wages prevail. It must be remembered, however, that some workers pay half their wages in taxes.

Energy

Oil and natural gas are mined from platforms in the North Sea. These platforms produce some 171,000 barrels of crude oil a day. The oil is both sold within Denmark and exported. There is always a risk involved when mining oil from the sea. A break in an underwater pipeline can pollute the ocean. In Denmark, surrounded by the sea, such a break could be disastrous.

Wind power is a cleaner, safer way to produce energy. Denmark is a world leader in the use of windmills. Harnessing the wind makes sense in a flat land such as Denmark, where breezes

constantly flow from sea to shore. Danish companies began building modern windmills to generate electricity in the 1970s. By 2015, wind power produced about 42 percent of the country's electricity. Denmark uses the highest proportion of wind power of any nation in the world. Huge Danish-based companies, Vestas and Siemens Wind Power, make efficient wind turbines and sell them abroad. Many of the windmills Americans see whirling in the countryside were made in Denmark. More than twenty thousand Danes work in the wind turbine industry.

A Danish worker walks on an oil platform in the North Sea.

Transportation

To get around the small country, the Danish government encourages people to use mass transit rather than automobiles. Passenger service on trains is efficient and comfortable.

Both cars and trains cross the Oresund Bridge between Denmark and Sweden.

Driving in Denmark is an expensive way to get around, but bicycling is free, fun, and convenient. The country has 4,300 miles (7,000 km) of dedicated bicycle lanes. A flat countryside means riding a bike is an easy way to travel. About 500,000 bicycles are sold in Denmark each year. On average, each person in Denmark bikes about 1 mile (1.5 km) a day.

Meanwhile, owning and driving a car is expensive. For example, there is 150 percent sales tax when a person buys a new car. This means it costs $50,000 to drive a $20,000 new car off the car lot. And it costs almost $1,500 for a teenager to take a driver's license test.

Denmark's geography means that travelers must cross many bridges. The longest is the Oresund Bridge, which connects Denmark with Sweden. Completed in 1999, the 10-mile (16 km) bridge spans the rugged North Sea. Car drivers pay a fee of $37 to cross the bridge. Another engineering masterwork is the Great Belt Fixed Link, which connects the island of Zealand with the island of Funen. The Great Belt Fixed Link is a series of bridges and tunnels that took more than ten years to build and opened in 1998. One span in the Great Belt system is a 4-mile (6.5 km) suspension bridge, the second-longest suspension bridge in the world.

The nation's biggest airport is the Copenhagen International Airport, which serves more than 18 million passengers each year. Twenty-eight smaller airports also operate in Denmark.

CHAPTER 7

Old Danes, New Danes

NEW YORK CITY, THE MOST POPULOUS CITY IN the United States, is home to more than eight million people. The entire nation of Denmark, in contrast, has fewer than six million people. The nation ranks 116th in population among the world's 192 nations.

About 88 percent of all Danes live in cities and towns. Some people, however, live on tiny islands, isolated from the outside world. In order to shop or attend school, they must travel by ferry to reach larger islands or the mainland.

Opposite: **A bustling square in Copenhagen. More than one out of every three people in Denmark live in the Copenhagen metropolitan area.**

Old Danes, New Danes **79**

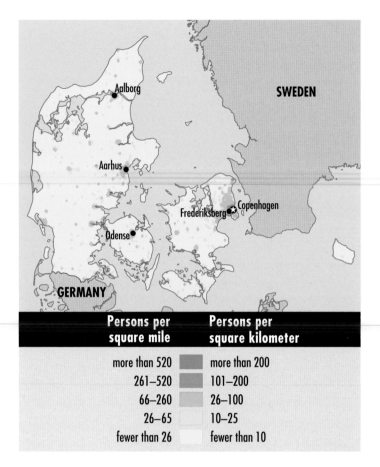

Persons per square mile		Persons per square kilometer
more than 520		more than 200
261–520		101–200
66–260		26–100
26–65		10–25
fewer than 26		fewer than 10

Who Are the Danes?

It is often said that Denmark is a homogeneous nation. This means that most people share a similar background and set of values.

Ethnic Danes are the descendants of the tribal peoples who settled Jutland and the neighboring islands in the sixth century. The Danish royal family traces its ancestry back to the ninth century and perhaps even earlier.

A person does not have to come from an ancient Danish family in order to be considered a Dane. It is often said that to be Danish is to speak the Danish

Greenlanders and Faroese

People who live in Greenland and the Faroe Islands are full Danish citizens. An estimated nineteen thousand Greenlanders and twenty-three thousand Faroese live in Denmark today. Many of these people speak their native languages—Greenlandic and Faroese. Greenlandic is a blend of Danish and Inuit languages, spoken by the native people of the area.

language and to have a Danish outlook on life. In general, Danes embrace the values of cooperation and lifelong learning. The ability to work well with others is highly regarded. A teacher in West Jutland explained, "Each individual should be developed in his or her own way—but also should know how to function within a group. You have to be personally enlightened to enable you to be part of the democracy we have today."

Population of Major Cities (2016 est.)

Copenhagen	591,481
Aarhus	264,716
Odense	175,245
Aalborg	112,194
Frederiksberg	104,481

Workers and Refugees

About 12 percent of the people in Denmark are immigrants or the children of immigrants. An immigrant is defined as someone who moved to Denmark from another country and does not hold Danish citizenship.

About half the immigrants to Denmark come from another European nation. The largest group of European immigrants is from neighboring Norway and Germany. There are also many immigrants to Denmark from the Middle East, Asia, Africa, and Latin America.

Immigrants have played an important part in Danish life for hundreds of years. In the 1600s, King Christian IV invited Jewish people from several European countries to

Denmark's Ethnic Groups

Danish	90%
Asian, African, Middle Eastern	7%
Other European	3%

People have immigrated to Denmark from all over the world.

settle in Denmark because he believed that the immigrants would contribute to the nation's cultural life and strengthen its economy. In the nineteenth and early twentieth centuries, the government invited workers to enter Denmark from Germany, Poland, and Sweden. Thousands of these immigrants took jobs in Denmark's potato and turnip fields. Within a few generations they blended into Danish society.

In the 1960s and early 1970s, Denmark welcomed about fifteen thousand immigrants from Turkey, Pakistan, Morocco, and Yugoslavia as "guest workers." These men and women took low-paying jobs in factories, on construction crews, and on farms.

By the late twentieth and early twenty-first centuries, growing numbers of people were fleeing war and famine in Africa and the Middle East. Driven from their native lands by disastrous conditions, millions of these refugees sought to establish new homes in Europe.

New Danish citizens gather for a celebration in 2016.

In the years after World War II, Denmark welcomed refugees from other European nations. In the twenty-first century, however, many people in Denmark grew less friendly toward newcomers from other lands. They feared that Muslim refugees from such countries as Iraq, Syria, and Lebanon would not fit into Danish society. Some Danes feared that the newcomers' customs would be too different from their own. In addition, some politicians argued that the newcomers put a strain on Denmark's schools, health care services, and other government programs.

In 2015, more than a million refugees fled to Europe to escape their war-torn homelands in Africa and Asia. In Denmark, the largest numbers of refugees came from Syria and Afghanistan.

Compared with such countries as Germany and Sweden, Denmark received relatively few refugees. In 2013, 6,184 people sought asylum in Denmark. In 2015, however, the number of new asylum seekers rose to more than 10,000.

In 2015, the Danish government passed a series of laws designed to make Denmark less appealing to immigrants. Immigrants were required to turn over most of their money to the Danish authorities. The new laws made it more difficult for family members to join refugees living in Denmark. One town even passed a law that encouraged the public schools to serve pork in school lunches. Since followers of Islam do not eat pork, this ordinance was hostile toward Muslim families.

As more refugees settled in Denmark, they called for full integration into Danish society. They pointed out that they

Some Danes have objected to the influx of immigrants. Others (above) have welcomed the newcomers, protesting the nationalists who would keep them out.

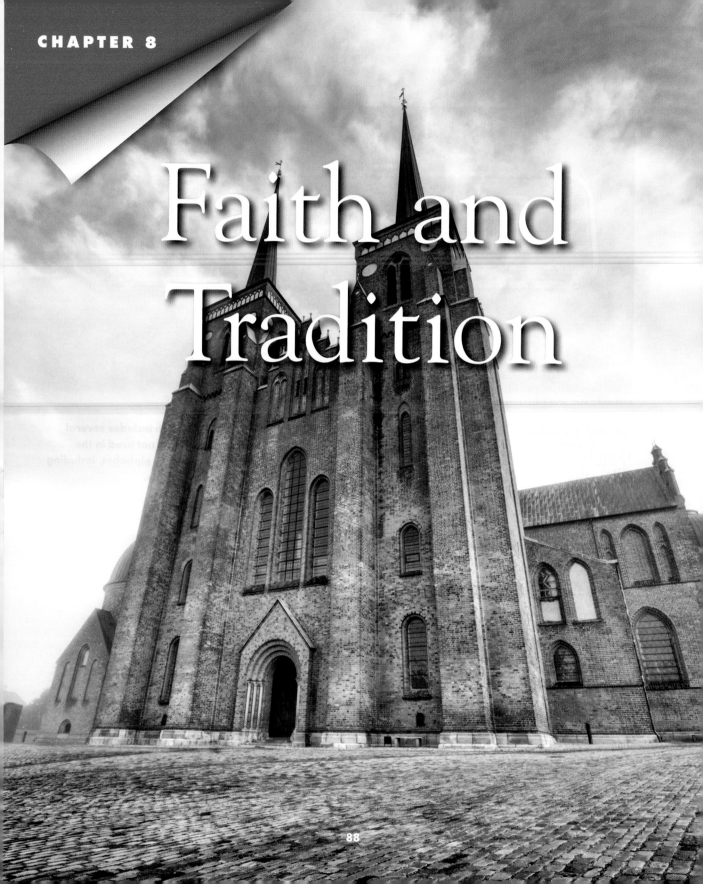

CHAPTER 8

Faith and Tradition

AT THE END OF EVERY SUNDAY SERMON IN THE Evangelical Lutheran Church of Denmark (ELCD), the pastor offers a special blessing. He or she blesses the queen and the royal house of Denmark. The ELCD is known in Danish as the Danske Folkekirke, or Danish People's Church.

The National Church

The Danish constitution declares the ELCD to be the national church of Denmark. The constitution also states that the nation's monarch must be an ELCD member. About 12 percent of the church's revenue comes from the Danish government. It is the only church in the nation to receive government funding.

Opposite: **Construction began on Roskilde Cathedral on Zealand in the 1100s. It is the oldest Gothic cathedral made out of brick.**

Frederick's Church in Copenhagen is known as the Marble Church.

In 2015, 78 percent of all Danes belonged to the ELCD. Few people attend church services regularly, however—only about 5 percent. Most Danes go to church only for family occasions such as weddings and funerals, and perhaps on holidays.

Tombs of the Monarchs

Roskilde Cathedral in the province of Zealand has been the burial site for Denmark's kings and queens since the 1400s. The oldest part of the cathedral was built in about 1100. New sections have been added over the centuries whenever the royal family needed more space for its graves. The most recent addition, completed in 2013, is the future burial place of Queen Margrethe and her husband.

Women and the Church

The Evangelical Lutheran Church of Denmark began to ordain women as pastors in 1948. However, the first female bishop was not ordained until 1995. Some male pastors strongly resisted serving under a female bishop. As more women became bishops, however, resistance gradually faded.

Denmark is divided into ten church districts, or dioceses, and another is based in Greenland. Each diocese is headed by a bishop who presides over a cathedral. Every diocese is divided into several parishes. Parish pastors preach in the local churches, conduct weddings, and visit the sick and dying.

An Evangelical Lutheran bishop baptizes a member of the royal family at Fredensborg Palace.

Pakistani immigrants in Copenhagen pray during Ramadan, the holiest time of the year in the Muslim calendar.

Freedom to Worship

Although Denmark has a national church, the Danish constitution ensures freedom of religion throughout the land. In addition to the Folkekirken, Danes follow many other faiths. Roman Catholicism was forbidden in Denmark from 1536 until the middle of the nineteenth century. Today, Denmark is home to about forty thousand Roman Catholics, most of whom are immigrants from eastern Europe.

In addition to the ELCD, Danes belong to several other Protestant churches. Among these are the Baptist Church of Denmark and the Reformed Synod of Denmark. The first missionaries from the Church of Jesus Christ of Latter-day Saints, or the Mormon church, visited Denmark in 1850. Many Danish converts to Mormonism emigrated to the United States and helped build the Mormon community in Utah.

Jewish people have lived in Denmark since the seventeenth century. Today, three synagogues, Jewish houses of worship, hold services in Copenhagen.

Muslims, followers of the religion Islam, first came to Denmark in the 1960s, when the Danish government invited immigrants from Turkey to enter the country as guest workers. Another wave of Muslims arrived in the 1990s and in the early twenty-first century. These Muslims came as refugees from Syria, Lebanon, Somalia, and other war-torn countries. About 3 percent of all Danes are Muslims.

Religion in Denmark (2012)

Evangelical Lutheran Church of Denmark	80%
Islam	4%
Other or none	16%

Lutherans celebrate Easter outdoors at a church in Copenhagen.

Celebrations Through the Year

Many of Denmark's religious celebrations revolve around Easter. The exact date of Easter varies depending on the position of the moon, but it always falls on a Sunday in the spring, sometimes between March 22 and April 25.

Shrovetide, a favorite holiday among Danish children, is celebrated forty days before Easter. During this holiday, bakeries feature special cakes called Shrovetide buns. Children dress in colorful costumes and go from house to house, asking for coins and treats. When someone opens the door, the children sing, "Buns up, buns down, buns in my tummy. If I don't get any buns, I'll make trouble."

A game played at Shrovetide is called Cat in the Barrel. A barrel filled with candies hangs from a rope, and children swing a heavy stick to break it open, much as children break open piñatas in North America. The child who breaks the barrel is called the King or Queen of Cats. This game dates

A boy dressed up in costume whacks a barrel during Shrovetide.

Elaborately decorated eggs are an Easter tradition in Denmark.

back to the 1500s, when people believed that cats were witches' pets. A live cat was hidden in the barrel instead of candy. When the barrel broke and the cat dashed away, it was thought that evil spirits fled from the village.

Easter itself is celebrated as a time of rebirth and renewal. People plant gardens and decorate their homes with flowers. Green and yellow are the traditional Danish Easter colors. The egg is an important Easter symbol in Denmark, just as it is in North America.

Great Prayer Day takes place on the fourth Friday after Easter. Choirs perform and church bells peal. Families take walks to enjoy the spring weather. Hot wheat buns are a special Prayer Day treat.

In the fall, an important celebration is All Saints' Day, on November 1. On the eve of the holiday, families place candles on the graves of their deceased relatives. In recent years,

In recent years, Halloween has become a popular tradition in Denmark, celebrated much like it is in the United States.

Gift-giving is a traditional part of the Danish celebration of Christmas.

Danish children have adopted the North American custom of going trick-or-treating on the evening before All Saints' Day, known in the United States as Halloween. They even shout "Trick or treat!" in English when a neighbor opens the door.

The month of December is filled with excitement over Christmas. Danes celebrate Christmas by decorating their homes with evergreen branches and ornaments. Stores are

filled with toys and other displays, and children make lists of the gifts they hope to find on Christmas morning. Many families attend church services on Christmas Eve, where they sing Christmas carols.

Ramadan, one of the major holidays in the Muslim calendar, occurs throughout the ninth month of the Muslim year. Because the Muslim calendar is eleven days shorter than the Western calendar, Ramadan falls about eleven days earlier each year. During Ramadan, Muslims fast, or do not eat, from sunrise to sunset. Ramadan is a time of prayer, humility, and charity. After sunset, friends and families gather for feasting and fellowship. Since sunset may not come until 10:00 or 11:00 p.m. during Denmark's summer months, Danish Muslims are allowed to break their fast earlier in the day.

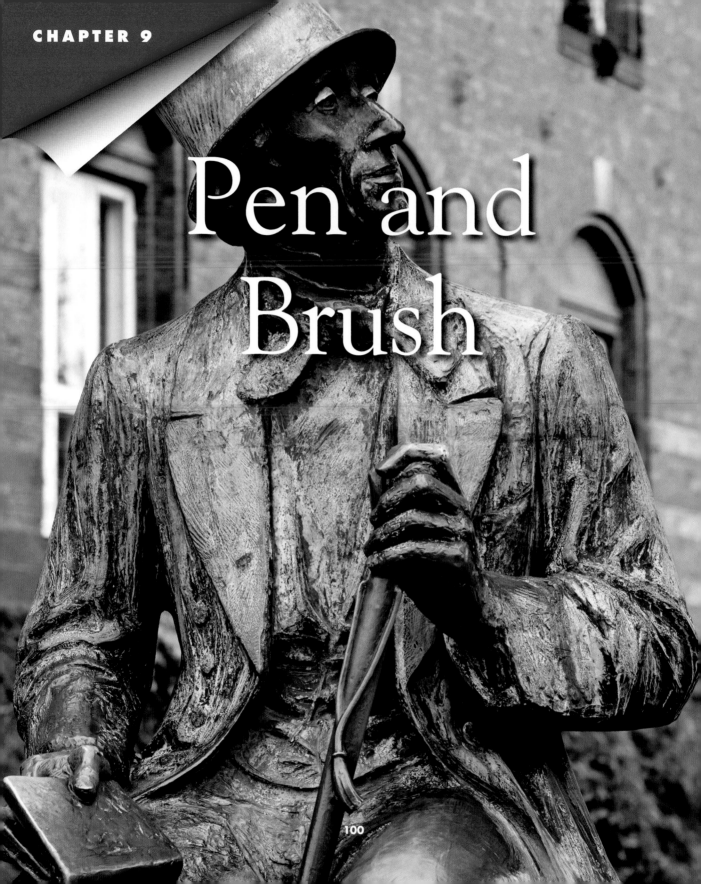

CHAPTER 9

Pen and Brush

THOUGH DENMARK IS A SMALL COUNTRY, IT STANDS tall on the world stage when it comes to the arts. Danish writers, artists, and architects are admired around the globe.

The Power of the Pen

Because the number of Danish speakers is relatively small, most Danish writers dream of finding an audience beyond their country's borders. Some choose to write in English, German, or French in order to reach more readers.

Hans Christian Andersen is known the world over as the creator of "The Ugly Duckling," "The Emperor's New Clothes," "The Little Mermaid," and countless other beloved tales for children. Andersen was born in the town of Odense and

Soren Kierkegaard was one of the most influential philosophers of the twentieth century. He was highly critical of the religious establishment.

moved to Copenhagen at age fourteen. Although he wrote several novels and travel books for adults, those works are nearly forgotten. His fairy tales, however, have been translated into nearly 150 languages.

Every student of philosophy is familiar with the work of Soren Kierkegaard. A native of Copenhagen, Kierkegaard filled seven thousand pages of journals with his thoughts about ethics, decision making, Christian principles, and more. His writings often include a dialogue between two characters with opposing points of view. Kierkegaard is the founder of the philosophical school of thought called existentialism. Existentialism argues that humans act as individuals, directing their own lives.

Karen Blixen, born in 1885, moved with her husband in 1913 to Kenya, where they established a coffee plantation. Writing under the pen name Isak Dinesen, Blixen described her Kenyan years in a memoir called *Out of Africa*. Returning to Denmark in 1931, she wrote several collections of short stories including *Seven Gothic Tales* and *Winter's Tales*.

Though Karen Blixen was Danish, she wrote most of her work in English and then translated it into Danish.

Resistance and Revival

One of Piet Hein's poems, published soon after Germany invaded Denmark in World War II, is a coded story of loss and resistance. It says that when freedom is lost one must fight back in order to be complete when freedom is finally regained.

Losing one glove
is certainly painful,
but nothing
compared to the pain
of losing one
throwing away the other
and finding the first one again.

One of Denmark's most powerful poets was also a scientist, mathematician, and inventor. Piet Hein invented an oval building form that became the basis for much of Denmark's modern architecture. Hein's short, clever poems began to appear in Danish newspapers during the German occupation of World War II. Many of these poems had hidden meanings. The Danes understood the message, but it slipped past the German censors.

Tove Ditlevsen grew up amid poverty in the slums of Copenhagen after World War I. Memories of her unhappy childhood haunt her novels, stories, and poetry. Her memoir *Early Spring* portrays the anguish of growing up female in a world where opportunities for girls were almost nonexistent. The women's rights movement of the 1970s hailed Ditlevsen as a champion of women's freedom. The opening line of *Early Spring* carries the message of possibility: "In the morning there was hope."

The frescoes at the Fanefjord Church cover the arches of the ceiling.

Silver, Clay, and Canvas

After the Protestant Reformation, Denmark closed its Roman Catholic churches and suppressed the religious works of art that had been created over the previous centuries. The paintings in many churches were destroyed, but others were simply covered with layers of whitewash. During the nineteenth and twentieth centuries, hundreds of these hidden paintings were rediscovered and restored. Today, these paintings can be seen in some six hundred Danish churches. Among the most famous are the fifteenth-century paintings by the Elmelunde Master in

Jorn Utzon's Bagsvaerd Church is considered one of the greatest modern churches.

Kennedy and Richard M. Nixon in their televised debate in 1960. This chair helped make Danish modern furniture popular in North America.

The Royal Danish Academy of Fine Arts has also produced a number of world-renowned architects. After completing his studies in 1942, Jorn Oberg Utzon traveled the world, studying building styles wherever he went. He was especially impressed by the pyramids built by the Maya people of Mexico. In 1957, he won a competition to design an opera house in Sydney, Australia. With an extraordinary roof that looks like shells or sails, the Sydney Opera House is one of the world's most recognizable buildings. One of Utzon's outstanding works in

Denmark is Bagsvaerd Church north of Copenhagen, which was completed in 1976.

Another innovative Danish architect, Bjarke Ingels, graduated from the Royal Danish Academy of Fine Arts in 1999. His works include a large, magnificent apartment complex shaped like a figure eight that stands in Copenhagen. Ingels and his team also designed the remarkable Lego House in Billund in 2013. Sections of the house resemble Lego pieces, and a child could build a miniature version of the real thing.

The work of architect Bjarke Ingels breaks the rules of what buildings are supposed to look like. Ingels designed this pavilion as part of an art gallery exhibition in 2016.

The Joy of Music

Denmark has a long musical history. During the Middle Ages, farmers called their cows by playing notes on a long horn called a *lur*, or birch trumpet. Archaeologists have found some thirty-five examples of bronze lurs at sites in Denmark. About 3 feet (1 m) in length, the bronze lur has no finger holes for changing the notes. The player used his or her lips and tongue to adjust the pitch.

By 1519, the royal court had its own court singers and a small orchestra. King Christian IV, in his eagerness to bring culture to Denmark, brought foreign musicians to the country so that local players could get the best possible instruction.

A statue in Copenhagen shows two men playing lurs. The oldest lur found in Denmark dates back more than two thousand years.

During Denmark's Golden Age, Christoph Ernst Friedrich Weyse composed carols, hymns, and secular songs called *lieder*. Weyse became the official court composer in 1819. Hans Christian Lumbye was the first music director at Tivoli,

Copenhagen's famous amusement park. His most popular piece is "Champagnegaloppen," or "Champagne Gallop." This lively tune opens with the pop of a champagne cork.

The music of Carl Nielsen is performed today by symphony orchestras throughout the world. Nielsen grew up in a village on the island of Funen, where he learned folk songs that people had sung for hundreds of years. The first of his six symphonies premiered in Berlin in 1896. Nielsen's Fourth Symphony is the most widely performed today. Another work by Nielsen, *Maskarade*, is considered Denmark's national opera.

A number of rock musicians have built reputations within and outside of Denmark. Lars Ulrich, a drummer who cofounded the band Metallica, became the first Dane to be inducted into the Rock and Roll Hall of Fame.

Carl Nielsen is considered Denmark's greatest composer. He was also a violinist and conductor.

CHAPTER 10

Fun and Family

BECAUSE DENMARK LIES SO FAR NORTH, WINTER DAYS are short and winter nights are long. Winter weather is cold, windy, and damp. Nevertheless, the Danes have learned to make the most of this uninviting climate. During the winter they gather in warm kitchens to share meals, tell stories, and play games. The Danish word *hygge* speaks to the snugness of kitchens on winter nights. It conveys the warmth and togetherness of the Danish home. It also involves a spirit of cooperation that is central to Danish society.

Opposite: **Watersports such as kayaking are popular in Denmark.**

A *kransekage*, a traditional Danish wedding cake, consists of a stack of rings of cake held together with icing.

At Home

Danish families are generally close-knit and supportive. Danes are very warm and welcoming to members of their extended families. They sometimes host "cousin parties" for their near and distant relations. Birthdays, weddings, christenings, anniversaries—any event is an opportunity to get everyone together.

To people outside the family, however, Danes sometimes can seem more distant. Acquaintances do not drop in on each other unexpectedly. In fact, people may know each other for years before they visit one another's homes.

Celebrating Together

Danish families celebrate many holidays together. The new year begins with the striking of the clock on Copenhagen's Town Hall, broadcast throughout the land. Danes welcome the year with noisemakers and balloons. They decorate their homes with streamers, put on funny hats, and eat a special New Year ring cake made of almond-flavored pastry called marzipan.

Liberation Day, celebrated on May 5, commemorates the day in 1945 when Denmark was liberated from the German occupation. On this day, Danes place lighted candles in their

Danes drive a German military vehicle into the town of Frederikshavn during a reenactment of the liberation of Denmark from German occupation during World War II.

Fireworks light up the sky above Copenhagen during a New Year's Eve celebration.

windows. June 5, Constitution Day, marks another important anniversary in Denmark. It commemorates the day in 1849 when Denmark became a constitutional monarchy. Valdemar's Day, June 15, is the national flag day. People buy miniature flags to decorate their homes.

November 10 is a time of family gathering called Martinmas Eve. Duck or goose is the traditional meal.

The year closes on New Year's Eve with the Monarch's Speech, broadcast at 6:00 in the evening. The Monarch's Speech was first broadcast in 1942 when King Christian X addressed the nation, calling upon Danes to keep their spirit and resist the enemy.

National Holidays

New Year's Day	January 1
Maundy Thursday	March or April
Good Friday	March or April
Easter	March or April
Prayer Day	April or May
Ascension Day	May
Pentecost	June
Constitution Day	June 5
Christmas Eve	December 24
Christmas	December 25
Day after Christmas	December 26

Learning for Life

About 70 percent of all Danish women work outside the home. For this reason, most Danish children attend child-care centers by the time they are six months old. From a very early age, they learn to play well together and to share with others.

By law, Danish children must complete nine years of schooling. At graduation, half of these students choose a trade and begin an apprenticeship. Some 30 percent enter a program to train for a profession such as teaching or nursing. About 20 percent of young Danes go on to one of the nation's five universities. A university education is free, but entrance exams are very challenging.

Learning does not end when formal education is over. Scattered across the country are seventy "folk schools" where adults can study art, literature, drama, philosophy, and a host of other subjects. The Danish government pays about half

A Danish teacher and students

of the cost, making the folk schools affordable for most who want to attend. The folk schools reflect the Danish belief that learning is a lifelong process.

Preacher, Teacher, and Poet

Nikolaj Frederik Severin Grundtvig is revered as the founder of Denmark's social philosophy, and is considered the founder of Denmark's folk schools. He was a poet and playwright, a pastor and philosopher, and a dedicated educator. He believed that schools and universities should educate people so that they could take an active part in the political process. He worked to encourage creativity and cooperation among students.

Back to the Land

Until the early 1990s, Danish food had a reputation for being filling but bland. Meals tended to be heavy on meat and starches such as bread and potatoes. In the 1990s and early 2000s, people in Denmark became interested in organically grown foods. Noma, a restaurant in Copenhagen, gave rise to new ideas about cooking and eating. Noma was rated the best restaurant in the world. Noma's chefs prepared delicious meals from locally harvested fruits and vegetables and locally caught fish. They even gathered wild mushrooms and collected wild

A chef puts a finishing touch on a dish of only local ingredients at the restaurant Noma.

herbs to season the dishes they prepared. They shared their ideas with chefs from other Scandinavian countries, creating a variety of cooking called the new Nordic cuisine.

Bread is still a central part of most Danish meals. Breakfast often consists of coffee or tea and rolls. The rolls are sometimes eaten with cheese or jam. For lunch, many Danes have an open-face sandwich called a *smorrebrod*, a thick slice of rye or whole wheat bread with a slab of herring, ham, or chicken.

Dinner typically includes meat and potatoes with vegetables or a salad. In recent decades, foods such as pasta and pizza have become popular.

A woman looks at the breads and pastries available at a bakery in Copenhagen. Rye bread is one of the most common types of bread in Denmark.

Mandelsmorboller

Desserts in Denmark often incorporate fruits such as apples or berries, and almond is a popular flavoring. Have an adult help you with this recipe for *mandelsmorboller*, delicious almond butter balls.

Ingredients

1 cup soft butter

3 tablespoons powdered sugar

1 teaspoon vanilla

¼ teaspoon almond extract

1½ cups flour

1 cup chopped almonds

Powdered sugar

Directions

Preheat the oven to 350°F. Mix the butter and sugar together. Add vanilla and almond extract, and then mix well. Stir in the flour. Add the chopped almonds to the mixture. Shape the dough into small balls and place them on ungreased cookie sheets. Bake the balls for about 20 minutes. Roll them in powdered sugar while they are still warm. Enjoy!

The Competitive Edge

Cooperation is a basic value in Danish life. When it comes to
sports, however, the Danes throw themselves into the spirit of
competition. About two million Danes actively participate in
sporting activities. Two-thirds of all children and teens belong
to teams or sports clubs.

Denmark's national sport is soccer. This sport is a passion
throughout Europe and much of the rest of the world. More
than three hundred thousand players actively participate in
soccer in Denmark. The game is played in schools at all levels,
from grade school through college.

When the Danish national soccer team won the European championship in 1992, the celebrations lasted for days. The biggest international soccer competition is the World Cup, which is held every four years. During the the World Cup, a strange hush falls upon the streets of Denmark. Stores close and cyclists and cars disappear. Everyone is inside, watching the games on TV. Denmark has never won the World Cup, but hope remains high.

Although Denmark is a small nation, it has done well

Fans gather in Copenhagen to watch the Danish national team play in the World Cup, the world's top soccer tournament.

Families enjoy a beautiful day at Tivoli Gardens.

in the Olympic Games. Since the first modern Olympic Games were held in 1896, Denmark has won forty-three gold medals (for first place), sixty-three silver medals (second place), and sixty-four bronze medals (third place).

Denmark is defined by the sea, and Danish athletes excel in water sports. Over the years Denmark has won six gold medals in rowing and twelve in sailing. Danish athletes have also excelled in canoeing, swimming, and boxing. Denmark is the only country ever to win three straight Olympic gold medals in women's handball.

Bicycling is a sport as well as a popular mode of transportation in Denmark. There are more bicycles in the country than there are people.

Chain Tag

Many traditional children's games enjoyed in Denmark build cooperation between players. In chain tag, two children run hand in hand to tag another child. The tagged child grabs a free hand, and the three run to tag someone else. The foursome then breaks into two teams of two. Those teams continue tagging and forming new teams until only one child is left. The last untagged child is the winner.

Some 3,000 miles (4,800 km) of designated bike trails and roads crisscross the country.

Other sports popular in Denmark are basketball, ice hockey, badminton, and golf. Since 1977, Danish players have won ten gold medals in the Badminton World Championships.

Fun and Games

Each year more than four million visitors flock to Tivoli Gardens, Copenhagen's world-famous amusement park. Founded in 1843, Tivoli is sometimes called the playground of Europe. The park has four roller coasters and the world's second tallest carousel, the Star Flyer, which lifts passengers 260 feet (80 m) above the city. Another popular ride is Aquila, a giant spinning swing. Tivoli also offers an aquarium, an open-air stage, and a concert hall that can seat 1,600 people.

From the top of the Star Flyer, a visitor to Tivoli can view all of Copenhagen spread out below. Ships bob in the harbor, and beyond roll the waves of the North Sea. This is Denmark—small in size, great in spirit.

Fast Facts

Official name: Kingdom of Denmark

Capital: Copenhagen

Official language: Danish

Aarhus

National flag

Official religion: Evangelical Lutheran Church of Denmark

National anthem: "There Is a Lovely Land" and "King Christian Stood by the Lofty Mast"

Type of government: Constitutional monarchy

Head of state: Monarch

Head of government: Prime minister

Area: 16,570 square miles (43,916 sq km)

Latitude and longitude of geographic center: 56° N, 10° E

Bordering country: Germany to the south

Highest elevation: Yding Skovhoj, 568 feet (173 m) above sea level

Lowest elevation: 23 feet (7 m) below sea level

Average high temperature: In Copenhagen, 36°F (2°C) in January, 72°F (22°C) in July

Average low temperature: In Copenhagen, 28°F (−2°C) in January, 57°F (14°C) in July

Average annual precipitation: 25 inches (64 cm)

Bornholm

Aalborg

National population (2016 est.):	5,593,785

Population of major cities (2016 est.):

Copenhagen	591,481
Aarhus	264,716
Odense	175,245
Aalborg	112,194
Frederiksberg	104,481

Landmarks:

- ▶ *Amalienborg Palace*, Copenhagen
- ▶ *Legoland Billund*, Jutland
- ▶ *Little Mermaid Statue*, Copenhagen
- ▶ *Mols Bjerge National Park*, East Jutland
- ▶ *Tivoli Gardens*, Copenhagen

Economy: Denmark has a highly developed economy based primarily on services. Trade is important to the economy, and the country exports more than it imports. Denmark extracts oil and natural gas from under the North Sea. The nation also has a thriving agricultural sector. Major products include wheat, barley, and hogs. Electronics, medicine, furniture, wood products, and windmill technology are all manufactured in Denmark.

Currency

Currency: Danish krone. In 2016, 1 Danish krone equaled US$0.15, and US$1.00 equaled 6.63 kroner.

System of weights and measures: Metric system

Literacy rate: 100%

Schoolchildren

Hans Christian Andersen

Common Danish words and phrases:

Hej	Hi
God morgen	Good morning
God nat	Good night
Tak	Thank you
Undskyld mig	Excuse me
Hvad hedder du?	What is your name?
Jeg hedder . . .	My name is . . .
Ja	Yes
Nej	No
Farvel	Good-bye

Prominent Danes:

Hans Christian Andersen (1805–1875)
Writer and storyteller

Karen Blixen (Isak Dinesen) (1885–1962)
Writer

Christoffer Wilhelm Eckersberg (1783–1853)
Painter

Soren Kierkegaard (1813–1855)
Philosopher

Carl Nielsen (1865–1931)
Musician and composer

Queen Margrethe II (1940–)
Queen of Denmark

Meet the Author

R. CONRAD STEIN IS THE AUTHOR OF more than two hundred books for young readers. He was born in Chicago, Illinois, when he became a fan of both libraries and the Chicago Cubs baseball team. At age eighteen, he joined the U.S. Marine Corps and served for three years. After his discharge, he attended the University of Illinois where he earned a degree in history. He then worked as a salesperson, a teacher, a social worker, and a truck driver while writing at night. Eventually, he was able to quit these jobs and write full-time.

Stein moved to Mexico, where he met his wife, Deborah Kent, who is also an author of children's books. They have a daughter, Janna, who is a special education teacher who instructs blind children.

To Stein, one advantage of writing history and geography books is it allows him to travel. He has traveled the world, and one of his favorite countries is Denmark. He enjoys the warmth and relaxed nature of the people.

Photo Credits